For my grandchildren
—M. E.

To my father, who closed his eyes and listened
—R. L.

ACKNOWLEDGMENTS:

I thank God for the comforting beauty of the arts.
The following resources were especially helpful:
Archives and Special Collections Library, Vassar College;
Teresa Carreño, "By the Grace of God," by Marta Milinowski;
Centro Cultural Teresa Carreño, Caracas, Venezuela;
and lapaginadeteresa.blogspot.com.
I'm deeply grateful to my husband,
Curtis Engle, and the rest of our family;
my wonderful agent, Michelle Humphrey;
amazing editor Reka Simonsen;
astounding illustrator Rafael López;
and the entire Atheneum/Simon & Schuster
publishing team.

ATHENEUM BOOKS FOR YOUNG READERS

An imprint of Simon & Schuster Children's Publishing Division
1230 Avenue of the Americas, New York, New York 10020

For information about special discounts for bulk purchases,
please contact Simon & Schuster Special Sales at 1-866-506-1949 or business@simonandschuster.com. • The Simon
& Schuster Speakers Bureau can bring authors to your live event. For more information or to book an event, contact
the Simon & Schuster Speakers Bureau at 1-866-248-3049 or visit our website at www.simonspeakers.com.
Book design by Semadar Megged • The text for this book was set in Caecillia.
The illustrations for this book were rendered in mixed media (acrylic on wood board, using sticks and other tools to
paint; watercolor; construction paper; pen; and ink), and then assembled digitally.
Manufactured in China • 0619 SCP • First Edition • 10 9 8 7 6 5 4 3 2 1
Library of Congress Cataloging-in-Publication Data
Names: Engle, Margarita, author. | López, Rafael, 1961- illustrator. | Title: Dancing hands : how Teresa Carreño
played the piano for President Lincoln / Margarita Engle ; illustrated by Rafael López. • Description: New York :
Atheneum Books for Young Readers, [2019] | Identifiers: LCCN 2018010123 (print) LCCN 2018011287 (ebook) | ISBN
9781481487412 (eBook) • ISBN 9781481487405 (hardcover) | Subjects: LCSH: Carreño, Teresa, 1853-1917—Juvenile
literature. | Pianists—United States—Biography—Juvenile literature. | Lincoln, Abraham, 1809-1865—Juvenile
literature. | Classification: LCC ML3930.C2635 (ebook) | LCC ML3930.C2635 E55 2019 (print) | DDC 786.2092 [B] —dc23 •
LC record available at https://lccn.loc.gov/2018010123

DANCING HANDS

HOW TERESA CARREÑO PLAYED
THE PIANO
FOR PRESIDENT LINCOLN

MARGARITA ENGLE ● RAFAEL LÓPEZ

A
atheneum

Atheneum Books for Young Readers

New York   London   Toronto   Sydney   New Delhi

WHEN TERESA was a little girl in Venezuela, Mamá sang lullabies while Papá showed Teresita how to let her happy hands dance across all the beautiful dark and light keys of a piano.

At first, making music seemed magical,
but Teresa soon learned that playing a piano
could be hard work. Sometimes she had to struggle
to make the stubborn music behave
as she practiced gentle songs
that sounded like colorful birds
singing in the dark and light branches
of a shade-dappled mango tree . . .
and powerful songs that roared
like prowling jaguars, beside towering waterfalls
in a mysterious green jungle.

If Teresa felt sad, music cheered her,
and when she was happy, the piano helped her
share bursts of joy. By the time she was six,
she could write her own songs, and at seven
she performed in the peaceful chapel
of a magnificent cathedral, playing hymns
that shimmered like hummingbirds.

Music was Teresita's delight, but suddenly
when she was eight, a war changed everything.
Guns blazed, swords flashed, and poor Papá
had to rush the whole family down to the seashore
and onto a ship, into a storm where wind howled,
waves rolled, barrels tumbled, ropes snapped,
and clouds bucked and kicked across the wild sky
like angry mules.

By the time the ship
arrived in New York,
Teresa felt lost. She was homesick.
How could she ever play happy songs again
in this unfamiliar country where
she did not know
a single friend?

Few people spoke Spanish, and all around her,
curious strangers stared and whispered,
as if her whole family belonged
in a museum
of oddities.

Worst of all, there was fighting here, too—
the horrible Civil War—North battling South
as soldiers marched and newspaper boys
hollered about victories, defeats, funerals,
and fears. . . .

Without a new piano,
Teresa would have felt even more lonely,
but soon she discovered that wherever one is,
some people are friendly, drawn together
by songs.

Musicians came to her home,
playing along while they listened
to the dazzling notes
of her dancing hands.

Determined to improve, Teresa practiced
graceful waltzes and sonatas,
booming symphonies, and lively folk songs,
her strong hands accepting the challenge
of life's many dark and light moods.

People began to call her the Piano Girl.
Her picture was in the newspaper
and on posters advertising concerts
where she performed with great orchestras
that invited her to play solos.

Teresa triumphed in enormous theaters
where children clapped and cheered
while their parents stood up and tossed roses.

With Papá at her side, she traveled
to elegant cities, and by the time she was ten,
the Piano Girl grew so famous that she received
amazing invitations, including one so special
that she could hardly believe her eyes—
President Abraham Lincoln wanted her to play
for his whole family at the White House!

But the country was still at war, so Teresa
arrived in Washington, DC, at a time
when freed slaves were signing up to be soldiers,
the injured moaned, and nurses groaned
from the sheer weariness of caring
for so many fevers
and wounds.

Not long ago the president's young son
had fallen sick, and had died.
Men argued about battles lost, battles won,
speeches made, victory delayed . . .
Teresa began to worry:
How could music soothe
so much trouble?

Poor Abraham Lincoln!
Teresa hoped she could entertain the president,
his grieving wife, and their two surviving sons.
Her fingers might stumble,
the rhythms emerging
too slow
or too fast.

But Teresa was brave, and she believed
in trying her best,
so she entered the White House silently,
clutching Papá's hand fiercely as they stepped
into a room so red that it looked like a storm
or a sunrise.

Teresa remembered how it felt to be
a homeless refugee, and how lonely she had been
surrounded by strangers, some of them rude
and others kind.

The memory of meeting past challenges
now helped her fingers dance, celebrating the way
life had turned out to be a mixture of all sorts of feelings,
happy and sad. But the piano was poorly tuned,
making her music sound ugly. What should she do?
Refuse to play?

She stopped, feeling discouraged, until Mister Lincoln
smiled kindly and asked for his favorite song,
"Listen to the Mockingbird."

Teresa knew she could play this lively piece
even on an imperfect piano, so her fingers
leaped across all the glorious dark and light keys,
improvising the way mockingbirds do, the melody
changing as she went along. Music swirled,
twirled, and soared on wings of sound.

The president listened quietly
to notes that rose, swayed, rippled,
and dipped like a bird in a blue sky
above a green forest.

He closed his eyes, nodded his head,
stretched his long fingers, and tapped
the tips of his shiny shoes.

When the joyful song ended,
Abe Lincoln stood up and clapped,
smiling at the Piano Girl, who smiled too,
because she knew that her music
had brought comfort to a grieving family,
at least for one brief, wonderful evening
of dancing hands.

From then on, Teresa felt certain,
she would always be bold enough
to share her musical courage
anywhere in the world,
simply by letting her fingers travel
across all the beautiful
dark and light
moments
of hope.

HISTORICAL NOTE

María Teresa Carreño García de Sena (1853–1917) was born into a musical family in Venezuela. Her father was a politician and amateur pianist who taught her how to play. By the time she was six, she was already composing her own music, and soon she was performing. In 1862, a revolution forced her family into exile. After they settled in New York, Teresa played at Irving Hall. She received several piano lessons from Louis Moreau Gottschalk, and in 1863, her original composition *Gottschalk Waltz* was published. She played as a soloist with the Boston Philharmonic and traveled to Cuba, where she performed to great acclaim.

In the fall of 1863, Teresa received an invitation to play for President Lincoln. He had already freed the enslaved people with his Emancipation Proclamation, and the Union had triumphed at Gettysburg. Saddened by the death of his son Willie, and worried about the future of the nation, Lincoln often took comfort in musical performances, including concerts by Teresa Carreño's teacher, Gottschalk.

After her White House performance, Carreño toured Europe, where she played for the famous composers Gioachino Rossini and Franz Liszt. Later tours took her all over the world, including Australia, New Zealand, and South Africa. She returned to Venezuela only once, because her countrymen disapproved of her, scandalized by the independent spirit that caused her to divorce three times before finding happiness with her fourth husband.

Teresa Carreño became known as a composer and opera singer, as well as one of the best pianists of her era, playing with such an intense spirit that audience members claimed they could hear the power of tropical nature in her music. She settled in Berlin, but returned to New York during World War I. Her remains, concert gowns, piano, and many of her documents were eventually returned to Venezuela, where she is remembered as La Leona ("The Lioness") of the piano.